MAGNIFICENT WILDERNESS

OREGON

STEVE TERRILL

FOREWORD BY JOHN DANIEL

WESTCLIFFE PUBLISHERS, INC. ENGLEWOOD, COLORADO

CONTENTS

Foreword	9
Preface	13
Wilderness Issues	18
Wilderness Map	20
Sky	22
Earth	36
Water	58
Plants	74
Trees	94
Technical Information, Acknowledgements	112

International Standard Book Number: ISBN 0-929969-41-3
Library of Congress Catalogue Card Number: 90-071517
Copyright, Photographs and Text: Steve Terrill, 1991.
   All rights reserved.
Copyright, Foreword: John Daniel, 1991
Editor: John Fielder
Assistant Editor: Margaret Terrell Morse
Production Manager: Mary Jo Lawrence
Map: Ann W. Douden
Typographers: Dianne Borneman and Ruth Koning
Printed in Korea by Sung In Printing Company, Ltd.,
   Seoul
Printing coordinated by Joanne Bolton, Bolton Associates,
   San Rafael, California
Published by Westcliffe Publishers, Inc.
   2650 South Zuni Street, Englewood, Colorado 80110

Bibliography

Specified quotes taken from *An Oregon Message* by William Stafford. Copyright © 1987 by William Stafford. Reprinted by permission of HarperCollins Publishers.

First Frontispiece: Rock formation at sunset,
   Bandon Beach
Second Frontispiece: Wild huckleberry and beargrass,
   Waldo Lake Wilderness, Willamette National Forest
Third Frontispiece: Mount Thielsen and
   thunderheads at sunset, looking toward
   Mount Thielsen Wilderness
Title Page: Foxglove and lupine on hillside,
   Clackamas County
Right: Larch trees, Monument Rock Wilderness

JOHN DANIEL

FOREWORD

Steve Terrill has gathered in this book the wealth of Oregon. From the bird rocks of Oregon Islands to Thielsen's spike to the bright granite shoulders of Eagle Cap, Rogue Valley and Columbia Gorge to the aspen canyons of Steens Mountain and the bare beauty of Leslie Gulch — there's a wild place for every spirit, for every mood that wants out of town. Old-growth Douglas firs and sparse steppeland junipers, bear grass and rabbit-brush, sword ferns and sage, it's all here. It's hard to speak of an Oregon landscape, we have so many. Rainforest, desert, sea coast, high meadow — nature had a lot in mind here, and didn't stint. A work of ages has made the land and is making it now, with volcanoes and glaciers, with basalt flows two miles thick, with rivers and breakers and the scouring of wind, with the growth and decay of forest generations building soil in the rain.

We're lucky to have such riches around us. It will take more than luck to keep them wild. My first experience in the Oregon back country came 20 years ago when a friend and I went hiking in Mount Hood National Forest. Two days along our trail, we saw light through the trees ahead — a big meadow, we thought, maybe a lake. The trail disappeared in a tangle of roots and boughs strewn across gouged muddy ground, studded here and there with a snapped-off trunk. The smell of sap was heavy in the air. We tried to pick up the trail, working around the far edge of the cut, but we never found it. After sitting for while in the wreckage, we turned back the way we had come.

I was new to the West and didn't know the term, but my friend and I had walked point blank into the practice of multiple use. Today, two decades later, it is painfully clear what the term means: enjoy yourself in whatever is left when the public lands have been stripped of their valuable commodities. If you stand on Mount Jefferson or Diamond Peak or any of the Cascade summits, you will see that a patchwork mange of clearcuts and roads has eaten into most of the expanse that was once all rolling green going blue in the distance. Or walk the desert of southeastern Oregon and observe the bright new forest there, the thousands of white plastic pipes that mark the ambitions of the next wave of public land extraction. There are specks of a yellow metal in that desert — a metal, as the Oglala seer Black Elk learned from bitter experience, that white people "worship and that makes them crazy." Crazy enough to turn a land upside down in heaps and holes, and to spray it with poison to leach the yellow stuff out.

The Oregon desert, like the Cascade woods my friend and I hiked, is open and available to the extractive exploitation of our human economy. By far, most of Oregon's public lands are open and available. They can't be bought, but they can be used, at cheap rates, in the hard ways that Americans have always used the windfall of the New World. The places that Steve Terrill shows you in this book are remnants, Oregon's share of the beautiful remnants of a wild country. Some of them are protected as designated wilderness and some are still vulnerable, badly in need of protection. For many of these threatened places, in a very few years the chance will be gone.

The Wilderness Act of 1964 established a new kind of boundary in our culture. It created the legal means to set aside parts of the land "where the earth and its community of life are untrammeled by man, where man himself is a visitor who does not remain." This boundary came

Left: South Sister reflects in Sparks Lake, Deschutes National Forest, looking towards Three Sisters Wilderness

into being because we have developed a way of life that makes it necessary. We have reduced the land to a mere platform for our human activities, an inconvenient expanse to travel across, and a storehouse — all too convenient — for the raw materials that fuel our growth economy. We have so engrossed the land, so carved it with the marks of our use and abuse, that we are in danger of losing it altogether in its original character. We are in danger of losing what it has to offer us besides timber and gold.

And what does it offer? What is it that refreshes us, skiing the winter stillness of Sky Lakes, or walking among Gearhart's big ponderosa pines, or rafting Owyhee Canyon? Surely, as Steve Terrill's photographs amply demonstrate, natural beauty is delighting to our eyes. Standards of beauty, though, are as changeable as culture itself. Mountains are beautiful today; three centuries ago they were "warts" and "beetling crags." Another value we attribute to wild places is peacefulness — one of our projects as a society seems to be to starve ourselves of solitude and quiet, and those lucky enough to know they are starving find sustenance in woods and desert. But though it may be found there, peace no more than beauty is what wilderness *is*. The prairie falcon gives no peace to the ground squirrel; rock and waves argue without end at Cape Lookout; Crater Lake and the other Cascade volcanoes testify to an explosive history driven by the relentless grinding of tectonic plates. Peace, and permanence too, are illusions of the nick of time we gaze through.

Then what is wilderness? What is it, deeper than beauty and peace and permanence, that we respond to? The word itself suggests an answer. In its old European roots, *wilderness* is related to the ideal of *willfulness*, the condition of being beyond control. Most of the world we have subjected to our human wants, but in wild places nature still works its unreckoned ways, ungoverned, undiminished, undisturbed. Its vast unconscious willfulness bodies forth mountains from seas of magma, dreams the dark chaos of soil skyward in forests of spring trees, fashions meadowlarks and black bears from the long weaving strands of evolutionary time. Walking in wilderness, we walk in rhythms longer than our conscious minds can know, a dance of ages that looks to us like stillness, sounds like deepest quiet.

And that, I believe, is what we love. Our delight is to join that dance again, if only for moments in our lives, to sense those ancient rhythms in which, in our small way, we belong. In wilderness we remember nature and ourselves — whatever our human world has become — as part of the old and original story that goes on. To draw a line around a wild place is first an act of self-restraint, a necessary limit on our human will, but finally it is an act of faith. Beyond this line, we say, a greater work goes on. This boundary preserves not only animals and trees, not only forests and river valleys, not only lakes and mountains and desert spaces. It preserves the possibilities of Earth.

— JOHN DANIEL

Left: Rhododendrons bloom beneath moss-covered hemlocks, Table Rock Wilderness

STEVE TERRILL

PREFACE

My journey started back in the early 1960s while sitting on a boulder fringed with emerald green moss. The top of the rock had been worn down over the years, presumably by other people visiting this same location on the Nestucca River. As I sat with fishing rod in hand, I heard the crystal-clear waters of the river as they swirled past my boulder, I saw sunbeams penetrate the early morning fog that lingered among the trees lining the river, I watched a water ouzel dart underwater, only to reappear downstream.

I had fished with my father many times before at this spot, but this day was somehow different. This was the day that marked the beginning of my love affair with the outdoors. This was the day that I realized that when I grew up I wanted to work outdoors, for the simple pleasure of taking in all of nature's beauty.

Perhaps it was because my father and I had caught our limit of fish that day. Or maybe my dad's speeches about respecting nature had finally sunk in. Whatever the reason, it was a day that I hoped would never end. I wanted nothing more than to remain in that spot forever.

My father passed away in 1979, just as I was beginning my photographic career. I wish he were alive today to see that I have been successful in my search for a meaningful profession that allows me to work in the great outdoors. I wish he knew that his love and understanding of nature have passed into my heart and my vision.

A few years after my father's death I returned to our old fishing spot on the Nestucca River. I was saddened by what I saw. Driving up the road alongside the river, I saw many more homes than I had expected, more logged areas, more land cleared for farming. My sense of anticipation mounted as I neared our magical spot. Reaching the stretch of river where I remembered it to be, I was dismayed to see the ugly hand of "progress" reaching out to me. The trees that once lined the river were gone. Land had been cleared across the river as well.

My boulder remained, however, and as I sat upon it, I realized that I still had my memories. No amount of progress can take them away from me. But will progress allow another father and son, another mother and daughter, to forge such memories on a boulder fringed with emerald green moss?

Since that memorable day, I have become more aware of the environment. I have immersed myself in the wilderness, taking time to simply appreciate the outdoors. Over the years it has become all too apparent to me that wild places will not last forever unless we take steps to protect our lands and waters.

Many areas of Oregon are already protected under various jurisdictions, but that doesn't mean they are completely sheltered from man's disturbance. I have seen much manmade destruction throughout our great state, including areas under protective designation. In addition to graffiti, littering, and vandalism of rock formations and rock art, there is the damage that comes from overuse. We must do more than simply legislate protection: we must teach people that these areas are fragile and unique — before it is too late. Otherwise we may be left with just our memories.

As my father taught me, I have taught my son to respect our earth. Over the years Steve has traveled with me many times and helped me capture on film many of the images in this book. One of our most memorable days together was during the summer of 1990.

Our plan was to spend a week in the Boulder Creek and Mount Thielsen wildernesses. I had studied the weather systems for the week ahead, and it looked as though the beginning of the week was going to be cloudy. The timing was right to hike in and photograph the view into Boulder Creek.

Steve dropped me off at the trailhead, as he often did, with the arrangement that he would pick me up at another trailhead at an agreed-upon time. If I was one hour late, he would begin to hike up the trail to meet me. Then we would decide if we wanted to spend the night in the wilderness or camp somewhere else.

I had planned to stay 10 hours in the wilderness, but after six hours the weather began to clear. Some

---

Left: Autumn leaves swirl at the base of Cabin Creek Falls, Columbia River Gorge National Scenic Area
Overleaf: Sunset over monoliths at Rainbow Rock, near Brookings, Oregon Islands Wilderness, southern Oregon coast

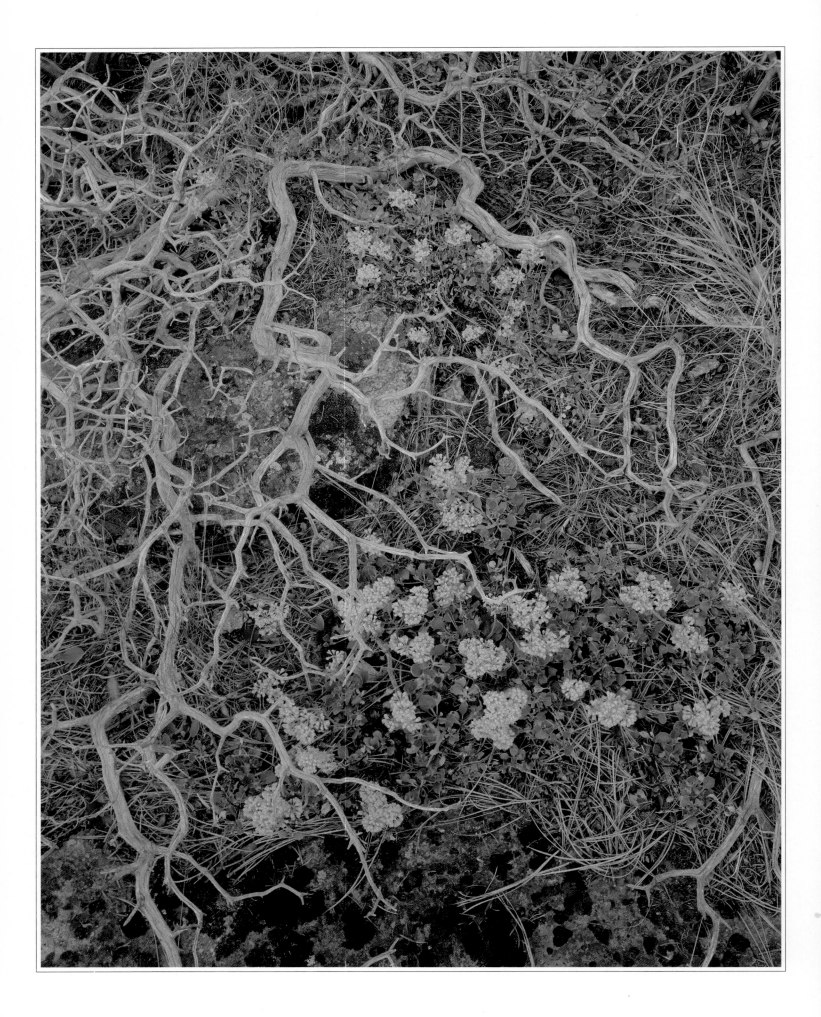

incredible clouds were building over toward Mount Thielsen, so I decided to head down to the trailhead and meet Steve early. This would give us enough time to drive to the Mount Thielsen trailhead and hike in a few miles to photograph the clouds over the mountain.

After packing up my camera gear, I hurried down the trail in — what was for me — record time. When I arrived at the parking lot, I didn't see Steve or the truck, so I figured he was either fishing, photographing or scouting other areas for me to photograph. With about two hours before our scheduled rendezvous, I remembered a dramatic basalt formation a few hundred yards from the trailhead on the other side of the North Umpqua River. Down the bank I went to the river's edge, just out of sight of the trailhead.

An hour later I finished shooting and headed back to see if Steve had arrived. The truck was there, but my son was nowhere to be found. Thinking he was fishing along the river while he waited for me, I too decided to wait. A half hour went by, then an hour, then an hour and a half. Since Steve is experienced in the wilderness, I wasn't worried about his welfare. What did bother me was whether he would return in time for us to get to Mount Thielsen.

Little more than an hour remained before sunset when Steve came running down the trail, carrying an apple and a bottle of cold water I later learned were for me. He had hiked up the trail early to tell me about the beautiful clouds that were building over Mount Thielsen. It wasn't until he saw my fresh footprints heading down a dusty section of trail that he realized I had already passed that way.

I threw my backpack into the truck and we took off for the mountain. The closer we came, the more intense the light became. Clouds were gathering in an ominous golden-orange layer that looked as if it were about to let loose a torrent of rain. Steve spotted a gorgeous rainbow to the east just as rain began to pound the truck. With little time left to photograph before sunset, we searched frantically for a vantage point to capture the rainbow and the mountain.

Stopping at a crest in the road, I threw on my backpack and took off running up the hill through the pouring rain. Steve was right behind me, with an umbrella and film in hand to feed my camera. Working as a team, we

mounted the camera on the tripod in two minutes. As the wind picked up speed, I considered giving up the shot. Steve encouraged me to continue.

I took his advice and covered my head with the focusing cloth. Intent on my work, I barely noticed a muffled crack and heavy thud that shook the ground nearby. When I asked Steve a few moments later what I had heard, he replied calmly that it was just a tree that had blown down 50 feet behind us!

Thank goodness there were only about 15 minutes left to shoot, or I probably would have retreated right then and missed the unbelievable sunset that was about to unfold. With the rainbow still high in the sky, the golden-orange we first viewed exploded into a vivid magenta that slowly faded into darkness.

As Steve and I trudged back to the truck in the driving rain, I realized that it was unlikely that I would have stayed around to photograph this breathtaking scene if we had met up at the trailhead in time to hike to the mountain. Even more important, I realized as I looked over at the grin on my son's face, we would have missed the opportunity to share an unforgettable experience.

I hope this book brings you to some pristine areas that you may not be able to reach on your own. Perhaps these images will awaken in you a deeper appreciation of wilderness, which you will pass on to others. For if we do not take steps now to protect our wilderness heritage, these pages may someday comprise a book of memories of what once was.

The journey that I began with my father along the Nestucca River continues today with my son. I, for one, do not want to deny my son the right to continue his own journey into wilderness. Our sons and daughters depend on us to preserve the world they live in. Let's not betray their trust.   — STEVE TERRILL

I dedicate this book to the memory of my father. Through his knowledge of nature, he taught me the wisdom of respect for our natural world.

Left: Sulphur flowers surrounded by dead manzanita, Badger Creek Wilderness

LARRY TUTTLE

WILDERNESS ISSUES

The first image I remember of my new Oregon home is the Siskiyou Mountains framed in the windshield of our 1954 pickup. Nothing could have looked more unlike the western Minnesota farmland of my birth. But one look convinced me that this was a land of unlimited wealth. To an 8-year-old, this meant visions of gold nuggets as large as my fist. Now, after 35 years of an unbroken, unabashed love affair with Oregon, I know that the wealth I was to discover is a different, rarer commodity. It is Oregon's bountiful and fragile wilderness landscape.

Fortunately for an innocent child in 1954, men of vision such as Aldo Leopold and Robert Marshall had already been at work to ensure that I would be able to share Oregon and the nation's wilderness wealth with my children and grandchildren. In 1930, Marshall wrote: "There is just one hope of repulsing the tyrannical ambition of civilization to conquer every niche on the whole earth. That hope is the organization of spirited people who will fight for the freedom of wilderness."

As U.S. Forest Service employees, Marshall and Leopold were successful in setting aside some areas from commercial development. These set-asides included the world's first wilderness preserve — New Mexico's Gila Wilderness — created in 1924 primarily through Leopold's efforts. Following World War II, however, the Forest Service was pressured to lift protection for these and the few other lands that had been protected as Wilderness.

These pressures prompted Wilderness Society leader Howard Zahniser to draft the Wilderness Act. The bill was first introduced into Congress in 1956. Eight years, 18 hearings and 66 versions later, Zahniser's shared vision became law, and 9.1 million acres were added to the nation's limited Wilderness Preservation System, including nine areas in Oregon.

Today, Oregon's 2,093,888 acres of designated wilderness are still less than 3.5 percent of the state's land area. Although 32 additions to Oregon's wilderness system have come in large omnibus bills in 1970, 1978 and 1984, successful designation of individual areas has always been the product of the efforts of determined groups of individuals, just as in Leopold and Marshall's time. The result is an unrivaled diversity of areas ranging from the 15 acres of critical wildlife habitat in the Three Arch Rocks offshore islands to the 358,461 acres comprising the Eagle Cap Wilderness.

The Oregon that most people know is well documented in this book: Mount Hood, Hells Canyon, Three Sisters, the Oregon Coast. This is the Oregon of temperate rainforests, unblemished coasts and snow-capped volcanic peaks. But there is another Oregon which comprises nearly three-quarters of the state's 96,000 square miles and is not well known even among Oregonians. The "other" Oregon is a land of immense vistas, fault-block mountain ranges, playas, lava-flow badlands, wind-carved ash and hidden rivers. The Great Basin leaves its indelible mark in southeastern Oregon, and parts of northeastern Oregon resemble the Rockies. Every area is imprinted with Oregon's unique stamp of wild beauty.

At this writing, lands from the "other" Oregon are the next to be added to the state's wilderness treasury. In 1991, the Bureau of Land Management will make a recommendation to Congress on new Oregon lands to be included in the wilderness system. The BLM is expected to recommend only a fraction of the four to five million acres conservationists believe deserve protection. These arid lands, among the most fragile in Oregon, are faced with intense extractive development pressures, such as uncontrolled off-road vehicle use and open-pit cyanide-process gold mining.

Comparatively speaking, the easy decisions establishing wilderness areas in Oregon have been or will soon be made. Large acreage additions are unlikely after designation of the BLM wilderness lands. However, some lands omitted for political reasons from previous wilderness proposals, such as Opal Creek, deserve protection and will be reconsidered. Some areas may be added as the result of congressional protection of the remaining ancient forest in the Pacific Northwest.

We are learning that the work of wilderness protection does not end with designation. Wilderness boundaries are often drawn as the result of political compromise and fall far short of addressing the need to protect the ecosystem in which the wilderness is located. A wilderness whose lakes are denuded of shoreline vegetation due to overuse by humans or livestock, or a wilderness surrounded by clearcuts or geothermal plants, is robbed of more than aesthetics. It is robbed of the core intention of the Wilderness Act, which is to be " . . . devoted to the public purposes of recreational, scenic, scientific, education, conservation, and historical use." Oregonians and all wilderness users must insist that the management of our public lands do more than create ecological islands. Wilderness can protect special and irreplaceable places, but wilderness alone cannot substitute for protection of the ecosystem.

Steve Terrill has provided a stunning, visual introduction to Oregon's wild places. Not all of these areas are protected. There will be many future battles to ensure that these lands, designated and undesignated, are not lost. Aldo Leopold in *A Sand County Almanac* reminds us "wilderness is a resource which can shrink but not grow. Invasions can be arrested or modified in a manner to keep an area useable for recreation, or for science, or for wildlife, but the creation of new wilderness in the full sense of the word is impossible."

— LARRY TUTTLE

EXISTING WILDERNESS AREAS IN OREGON

(All NFW except as noted)

BC — BADGER CREEK
BL — BLACK CANYON
BO — BOULDER CREEK
BR — BRIDGE CREEK
BW — BULL OF THE WOODS
CO — COLUMBIA
CC — CUMMINS CREEK
DP — DIAMOND PEAK
DC — DRIFT CREEK
EC — EAGLE CAP
GM — GEARHART MOUNTAIN
GK — GRASSY KNOB
HC — HELLS CANYON (USFS/BLM)
KM — KALMIOPSIS
MN — MENAGERIE
MS — MIDDLE SANTIAM
MC — MILL CREEK
MR — MONUMENT ROCK
MH — MOUNT HOOD

MJ — MOUNT JEFFERSON
MT — MOUNT THIELSEN
MW — MOUNT WASHINGTON
ML — MOUNTAIN LAKE
JD — NORTH FORK JOHN DAY
UM — NORTH FORK UMATILLA
OI — OREGON ISLANDS (BLM)
RB — RED BUTTES
RC — ROCK CREEK
RU — ROGUE-UMPQUA DIVIDE
SH — SALMON-HUCKLEBERRY
SL — SKY LAKES
SM — STRAWBERRY MOUNTAIN
TR — TABLE ROCK (BLM)
TA — THREE ARCH ROCKS (NWRW)
TS — THREE SISTERS
WL — WALDO LAKE
WT — WENAHA-TUCANNON
WR — WILD ROGUE (BLM/USFS)

WASHINGTON

Astoria

Seaside

Garibaldi

Pacific Ocean

N

Portland

The Dalles

CO

MH

SH

BC

Salem

5-6

5-1

5-8

TR

BW

5-9

Warm Springs

Albany

MS

MJ

Newport

Corvallis

DC

MN

MW

MC

BR

CC

Williamette River

RC

5-31

TS

Bend

5-34

5-3

Eugene

5-21

5-35

WL

5-42

5-43

OREGON

Coos Bay

Coos River

DP

1-2

1-3

1-24

BO

1-22

RU

Crater Lake National Park

MT

1-58

Roseburg

Summer Lake

Lake Abert

GK

12-8

WR

Rogue River

SL

GM

1-101

Cape Sebastian

Medford

Illinois River

ML

11-1

Klamath Falls

Drews Reservoir

OI

KM

12-14

RB

11-17

1-11

Goose Lake

Columb

Source: BLM & the Wilderness Society

CALIFORNIA

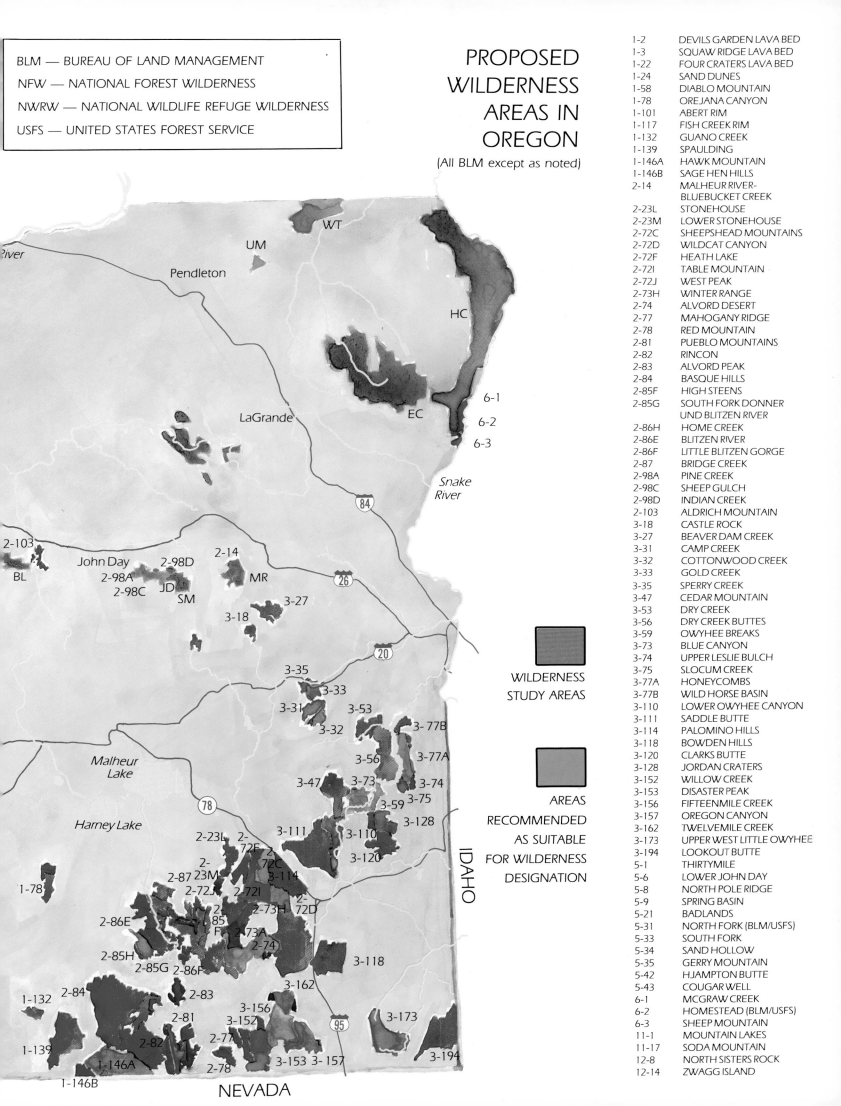

BLM — BUREAU OF LAND MANAGEMENT
NFW — NATIONAL FOREST WILDERNESS
NWRW — NATIONAL WILDLIFE REFUGE WILDERNESS
USFS — UNITED STATES FOREST SERVICE

PROPOSED WILDERNESS AREAS IN OREGON

(All BLM except as noted)

WILDERNESS STUDY AREAS

AREAS RECOMMENDED AS SUITABLE FOR WILDERNESS DESIGNATION

1-2	DEVILS GARDEN LAVA BED
1-3	SQUAW RIDGE LAVA BED
1-22	FOUR CRATERS LAVA BED
1-24	SAND DUNES
1-58	DIABLO MOUNTAIN
1-78	OREJANA CANYON
1-101	ABERT RIM
1-117	FISH CREEK RIM
1-132	GUANO CREEK
1-139	SPAULDING
1-146A	HAWK MOUNTAIN
1-146B	SAGE HEN HILLS
2-14	MALHEUR RIVER- BLUEBUCKET CREEK
2-23L	STONEHOUSE
2-23M	LOWER STONEHOUSE
2-72C	SHEEPSHEAD MOUNTAINS
2-72D	WILDCAT CANYON
2-72F	HEATH LAKE
2-72I	TABLE MOUNTAIN
2-72J	WEST PEAK
2-73H	WINTER RANGE
2-74	ALVORD DESERT
2-77	MAHOGANY RIDGE
2-78	RED MOUNTAIN
2-81	PUEBLO MOUNTAINS
2-82	RINCON
2-83	ALVORD PEAK
2-84	BASQUE HILLS
2-85F	HIGH STEENS
2-85G	SOUTH FORK DONNER UND BLITZEN RIVER
2-86H	HOME CREEK
2-86E	BLITZEN RIVER
2-86F	LITTLE BLITZEN GORGE
2-87	BRIDGE CREEK
2-98A	PINE CREEK
2-98C	SHEEP GULCH
2-98D	INDIAN CREEK
2-103	ALDRICH MOUNTAIN
3-18	CASTLE ROCK
3-27	BEAVER DAM CREEK
3-31	CAMP CREEK
3-32	COTTONWOOD CREEK
3-33	GOLD CREEK
3-35	SPERRY CREEK
3-47	CEDAR MOUNTAIN
3-53	DRY CREEK
3-56	DRY CREEK BUTTES
3-59	OWYHEE BREAKS
3-73	BLUE CANYON
3-74	UPPER LESLIE BULCH
3-75	SLOCUM CREEK
3-77A	HONEYCOMBS
3-77B	WILD HORSE BASIN
3-110	LOWER OWYHEE CANYON
3-111	SADDLE BUTTE
3-114	PALOMINO HILLS
3-118	BOWDEN HILLS
3-120	CLARKS BUTTE
3-128	JORDAN CRATERS
3-152	WILLOW CREEK
3-153	DISASTER PEAK
3-156	FIFTEENMILE CREEK
3-157	OREGON CANYON
3-162	TWELVEMILE CREEK
3-173	UPPER WEST LITTLE OWYHEE
3-194	LOOKOUT BUTTE
5-1	THIRTYMILE
5-6	LOWER JOHN DAY
5-8	NORTH POLE RIDGE
5-9	SPRING BASIN
5-21	BADLANDS
5-31	NORTH FORK (BLM/USFS)
5-33	SOUTH FORK
5-34	SAND HOLLOW
5-35	GERRY MOUNTAIN
5-42	H.JAMPTON BUTTE
5-43	COUGAR WELL
6-1	MCGRAW CREEK
6-2	HOMESTEAD (BLM/USFS)
6-3	SHEEP MOUNTAIN
11-1	MOUNTAIN LAKES
11-17	SODA MOUNTAIN
12-8	NORTH SISTERS ROCK
12-14	ZWAGG ISLAND

NEVADA

IDAHO

SKY

Endless in my mind and beauty to my eyes, the sky is an important element in every photograph I take. Even when it does not appear in an image, it has played an essential role by creating the light needed to capture a moment in time.

With the help of clouds, the sky produces nearly every shade in the color spectrum. As I look toward the heavens in the evening, the setting sun transforms the sky from blue to hues of yellow, orange, red and then back to blue, this time a midnight blue that darkens to black.

Many people don't like the kind of weather that produces rainbows, but I see it as an opportunity to capture magic in the sky. I cringe when I hear people describe a cloudless day as beautiful. I like character in the vast space above — puffy, wispy, ominous clouds, anything to give that big blue canvas some life.

As a photographer, I look toward the sky to plan my day. A beautiful sky interspersed with clouds signals landscape photography. When the sky is heavy with clouds and small patches of blue, I try to capture beams of light breaking through to spotlight subjects on earth. When the sky is completely filled with clouds, I turn my camera to the earth, where scenes are bathed in soft, even light.

Left: Evening light on the Painted Hills, John Day Fossil Beds National Monument   Above: Moccasin Lake at sunrise, Eagle Cap Wilderness

"More still than a star, one thought shies
by: what if the sky loved you?
But nobody knew? But that magnet in space
pulled hard? But you acted like nothing at all
was reaching or calling for you? More still
than a star going by, that thought stays.
A day at a time pieces of it glow. / Nobody notices: quiet days."
— William Stafford, "Say You Are Lonely"

Sunrise over Wizard Island, Crater Lake National Park

Rock formations and clarkia wildflowers in Leslie Gulch, Upper Leslie Gulch proposed wilderness
Overleaf: Fog at dawn over Cannon Beach, from Ecola State Park

"In the Aztec design God crowds / into the little pea that is rolling / out of the picture. / All the rest extends bleaker because God has gone away. . . .

Forest in fog along Varney Creek Trail, Mountain Lakes Wilderness

. . . In the White Man design, though, / no pea is there.
God is everywhere, / but hard to see.
The Aztecs frown at this.
How do you know He is everywhere?
And how did He get out of the pea?"
— William Stafford, "Ultimate Problems"

Rainbow and Mount Thielsen, looking toward Mount Thielsen Wilderness

"Spilling themselves in the sun bluebirds
wing-mention their names all day. If everything
told so clear a life, maybe the sky would
come, maybe heaven; maybe appearance and
truth would be the same. Maybe whatever seems
to be so, we should speak so from our souls,
never afraid, 'Light' when it comes,
'Dark' when it goes away." — William Stafford, "Simple Talk"

Sunrays penetrate morning fog, Wild Rogue Wilderness, Curry County

View of Wenaha-Tucannon Wilderness, from Lecture Point

"In the day I sheltered on the sunny side
of big stones. In the whole world other things
were giddy: they moved. I leaned on the steady part.

Every day passed into darkness. Dawn
rescued the top of the rocks and the middle
and then me. The sun loved my face. . . .

The aptly named Balancing Rocks, Deschutes National Forest

. . . You can hardly believe what I did: when winter / came,
when the nights began to be cold,
I dissolved away into the still part of the world.

Now it is cold and dark, and the long nights
return to the wilderness. One big rock is here
for my place. All else moves. I am learning to wait."
— William Stafford, "Afterward"

Eagle Cap Mountain reflects in Mirror Lake, Eagle Cap Wilderness
Overleaf: Evening light on Mount Hood, from the Nature Conservancy's Multorpor Fen, Mount Hood National Forest

EARTH

The earth holds much splendor, if you just look. Seeing the obvious beauty is easy: the immense cliffs of the Columbia River Gorge lined with trees and waterfalls, or late evening light bathing towering, snow-covered mountains that seem to glow with fire from within. Less obvious is the beauty of cracks in a dry lake bed, or river rock worn so smooth it seems to have been carved by the hand of man.

Since an early age I have been taught to respect the outdoors. We only have one Earth, my father would say, so take care of it. As a photographer I appreciate my father's words even more. Now that my eyes are trained to see earth's beauty, I see more and more being destroyed. The beauty I see in towering, lichen-encrusted columns of basalt, others may see as rock to be crushed for road fill. The beauty I see in a field of grasses and wildflowers, others may see as a great location for a housing development.

I have stood in wild places that seem almost sacred, as if I was the only person ever there. Such places allow me to experience the earth as it must have felt and looked before the dawning of man. Wherever I go, I plant my feet on this earth and my heart on this land.

Left: Columnar basalt along the North Umpqua River, Umpqua National Forest, near Boulder Creek Wilderness   Above: Natural basalt arch frames Saint Peters Dome, Columbia River Gorge National Scenic Area

"
. . . We felt a long slow wave / in the earth. It wasn't the
stars that moved, but ourselves,
in time to a dance the dead could feel. . . . / Crawling along
by a breath at a time, we tried to
get low; we tried to sight across level earth / near dawn and
let the time tell us about how
to be alive in the grass, the miles, the strangeness,
with only the sun looking back from the other end of light. . . .

Late evening light on Mount Hood, from Lolo Pass; Mount Hood National Forest

. . . We spread our arms out wide on the ground / and held
still. We set out for that cave we knew
above a stream, where early sunlight reaches / far back, willows
all around, and clams in the river
for the taking. And we prayed for that steady event / we had
loved so long without knowing it, our greatest
possession — the world when it didn't move."
— William Stafford, "Getting Scared"

Mount Hood pierces evening fog, from Lolo Pass, Mount Hood National Forest

"You put your hand on stone, for the coolness there, / and
how steady. It hasn't the wit of water, but you trust
it more. It will be there again tomorrow,
earning its place by not being anything else.
Remember the story of the bat? — hollering into
a cave, 'Anybody there?,' and a big rock
saying, 'Nobody but me,' and the others, 'But me,' 'But me,'
till the whole mountain had answered. That's how a rock is."
— William Stafford, "Stone, Paper, Scissors"

Trees echo the colors of lichen-covered basalt, Black Canyon Wilderness

Pacific silverweed and sandstone at Simpson Beach, Shore Acres State Park

Rare snowfall dusts the Oregon coast at The Three Graces, near Garibaldi

Snow blankets the Painted Hills, John Day Fossil Beds National Monument
Overleaf: White Butte from North Point, Bridge Creek Wilderness

"Any sun that comes, even
one not ours, could have these lakes
to drink out of, any time. / And other laws could come besides
the ones we have, all springing
from a force that makes them right.
The lives we have, while we have them,
can measure time, before and after
today, to use or give away. / On earth it is like this, a strange
gift we hold, while we look around." — William Stafford, "On Earth"

Pine needles surround lichen-covered basalt, Columbia Wilderness

Late evening light on Abert Rim, Abert Rim proposed wilderness

Shadow patterns in Little Blitzen Gorge, Steens Mountain, Little Blitzen Gorge proposed wilderness

Lichen- and snow-covered lava, Devils Garden Lava Bed proposed wilderness

"If anything ever happens to time again
let's crawl where we did that night in the cave
when both of us heard a star go by so still
that a crystal formed in our lives. Let's climb
that cavern the same slope as the hill but under
the hill, thus having the world as it is
but also shaped our way. . . .

Curly dock struggles along the receding edge of Hart Lake, Warner Valley

. . . Don't answer me now, it's too early; but listen —
I'm just talking about this, but see
what you think, later, when you have time:
we could stand there together and hear day coming,
and we could be neutral but welcome what came.
We could bow and hear the far-off world
that we knew, going away."

— William Stafford, "Something I Was Thinking About"

Three Sisters in Three Sisters Wilderness, from Panorama Point in Menagerie Wilderness

Last light of day on Steins Pillar, Ochoco National Forest, near Mill Creek Wilderness

Light patterns on rock pinnacle, Badger Creek Wilderness

"I listen, and the mountain lakes
hear snowflakes come on those winter wings
only the owls are awake to see, / their radar gaze and furred ears
alert. In that stillness a meaning shakes;
And I have thought (maybe alone
on my bike, quaintly on a cold / evening pedaling home),
Think! — / the splendor of our life, its current unknown
as those mountains, the scene no one sees."
— William Stafford, "Maybe Alone on My Bike"

Dry River in snow, Badlands proposed wilderness

Lone Douglas fir on hillside of pumice and eroded scoria formations, Rogue River National Forest, near Rogue-Umpqua Wilderness

"Next time what I'd do is look at
the earth before saying anything. I'd stop
just before going into a house / and be an emperor for a minute
and listen better to the wind / or to the air being still. . . .

And for all, I'd know more — the earth
bracing itself and soaring, the air
finding every leaf and feather / over forest and water . . . "
— William Stafford, "Next Time"

Hills bathed in morning light, North Fork Umatilla Wilderness

Lichen-covered boulders along Strawberry Lake, Strawberry Mountain Wilderness

WATER

Water is the lifeline of the earth. Winding, twisting, cutting through the land, it nurtures the life it holds within and gives life to its surroundings.

The power of water is a sight and sound to behold: glacial runoff terracing down mountains, surf pounding against coastal cliffs, dark summer clouds unleashing their fury upon the land.

I am intrigued by water's ability to change form as it moves across the land and through the seasons. Most dramatic, perhaps, is winter, when water crystallizes into snow, blanketing the land in white and transforming bleak scenes into magical landscapes. In winter, waterfalls and river spray create ice formations as magnificent as fine art in any gallery.

Water is essential to life itself, and to the life of many of my photographs.

Left: Millipede Creek tumbles down hillside, Table Rock Wilderness   Above: Ice formations along the Columbia River, Columbia River Gorge National Scenic Area

"Choose a day: whatever birds come
they're the ones, for this year.
If it's windy, multiply by two. (But what
if there's none, but might be? Mark *none*.)
Today there may be a song. Multiply:
'Two unknowns.' But you are always
the same, no matter how windy or cold
it is. You search all the thickets, then walk
home through the fields at the end: just one."
— William Stafford, "Bird Count"

Ice-covered lake in Seven Lakes Basin, Sky Lakes Wilderness

Waterfall at Hug Point State Park, northern Oregon coast
Overleaf: Snowy forest frames North Falls, Silver Falls State Park

"It's a place to go, far in the country,
unadvertised, where even the storms pass by.
Secrets there — that nobody wants to know —
rustle away; a bridge holds in stone with water-
sounds loud in spring and in summer low.
Deep in that golden light minnows play.
That's where I go every summer, because we lived there,
and wind, and space, and the hurt of space after
the others are gone, and my visit this one last time,
and the bittern's cry." — William Stafford, "Salt Creek"

South Fork of the John Day River cuts through South Fork John Day Canyon, border of Black Canyon Wilderness

Green waters of the Elk River, border of Grassy Knob Wilderness

"A flavor like wild honey begins / when you cross the river. On a
sandbar / sunlight stretches out its limbs, or is it / a sycamore,
so brazen, so clean and bold? / You forget about gold.
You stare — and a flavor / is rising all the time from the trees.
Back from the river, over by a thick / forest, you feel the tide of wild honey
flooding your plans, flooding the hours
till they waver forward looking back. They can't / return: that river divides
more than / two sides of your life. The only way
is farther, breathing that country, becoming / wise in its flavor, a native of
the sun." — William Stafford, "Looking for Gold"

Wild mint blooms along the Table Rock Fork of the Molalla River, border of Table Rock Wilderness

Evening light on rabbitbrush and boulders along the shore of Abert Lake, Lake County

"It happened to be Thursday. No one was going / to notice if I stopped
by home. Anyway, / now it was gone, covered by the lake that / came,
and marked with a plaque by the new road.
Here's where the house would be if I / had a son, if we owned the land,
if the lake / hadn't come. I tossed a rock in the air
for all that couldn't ever be, this time.
You know the power that falls through a wire / when a river falls? How
it wears for years / through its canyon? How you often come back alone?
How it turned into spray where it hit the stone?"
— William Stafford, "The Land Between the Rivers"

Still waters of Moccasin Lake, Eagle Cap Wilderness

Grasses line the North Fork of the John Day River, North Fork John Day Wilderness

"My father said, 'Listen,' and that subtle song
'Coyote' came to us: we heard it together.
The river slid by, its weight / moving like oil. 'It comes at night,'
he said; 'some people don't like it.' 'It sounds
dark,' I said, 'like midnight, a cold . . . '
His hand pressed my shoulder: / 'Just listen.' That's how I first
heard the song." — William Stafford, "Hearing the Song"

Rogue River cuts through Huggins Canyon, Wild Rogue Wilderness

"Now has come, an easy time. I let it
roll. There is a lake somewhere
so blue and far nobody owns it. / A wind comes by and a
willow listens
gracefully. I hear all this, every summer. I laugh
and cry for every turn of the world,
its terribly cold, innocent spin. / That lake stays blue and free;
it goes / on and on. / And I know where it is."
— William Stafford, "Why I Am Happy"

Diamond Peak reflects in Summit Lake at sunrise, Oregon Cascades Recreation Area,
looking toward Diamond Peak Wilderness

Surf pounds against sandstone cliffs, Devils Punchbowl State Park

Rushing waters of the Middle Santiam River, Middle Santiam Wilderness

PLANTS

The plant world is alive with colors, textures, shapes and scents. The kaleidoscopic hues of a fragrant field of wildflowers in full bloom will catch most people's attention. A forest saturated with hues of green usually doesn't have the same impact. It takes time to soak in the beauty of lacelike maidenhair ferns clinging to damp forest walls, of moss draping down from trees almost to the forest floor, of sword ferns protruding through a vividly green mosaic of wood sorrel.

In my photographic journeys throughout this great land, I rarely come across a landscape without some kind of vegetation. My photography is dependent on the beauty of plants, just as the American Indians were dependent on these same plants for food, medicine and dyes. Plants thrived on our planet long before man's arrival. And though plants can survive without man, man cannot survive without plants.

Left: Monkey flowers and lupine along Elk Cove Creek, Mount Hood Wilderness   Above: Cardwell's penstemon, Mount Hood Wilderness

Mount Washington and fall foliage near Big Lake, Willamette National Forest

Wild strawberry plants and alder leaves, Bull of the Woods Wilderness, Mount Hood National Forest

Rhododendron in bloom, Oregon Dunes National Recreation Area

Ferns and rhododendron, Bull of the Woods Wilderness

"Till the great darkness gathers them in / some time in the quiet after us / they have a secret life of their own / down there near the ground. . . . / In that long interval those . . . flowers begin to report. / Every night under my pillow the earth ticks / while somewhere in distant country tomorrow / wanders looking for me, and every morning / I go out and pat the ground again. Already / that comet with destiny in it has come by / a few times, but the years are still friendly. Certain . . . flowers hold on, hold on." — William Stafford, "Chicory"

Wood sorrel and sword ferns near the Salmon River, Salmon-Huckleberry Wilderness

Whitebark pine and Crater Lake currant, Crater Lake National Park   Overleaf: Indian rhubarb along Wild and Scenic section of the Illinois River, Kalmiopsis Wilderness, Siskiyou National Forest

"When we unfasten the cabin door in
the spring, an echo of our hammering
scares the blue jays, and all our section
of the country turns relevant for a while.
Summer days have been falling thousands
of years; they land quietly in the woods
at dawn and come forward with an embrace
like light on old faces in the family album. . . .

Evening primroses bloom at the base of Steens Mountain, looking toward High Steens proposed wilderness

... Writing their history in the sky, the last
of the summer birds go away. We hear
empty woods bravely surround our house
in open ranks, for autumn census, unafraid.
The storm that closes all the passes
just is — it doesn't come. It is as quiet
as in the story when the hunted wolf
wrestled with death in the hidden cave
and nobody ever found out who won."
— William Stafford, "Seasons in the Country"

Cattails and ice in McKee Basin pond, Sky Lakes Wilderness

Sumac begins its fall transformation, Hells Canyon Wilderness

Poison oak surrounded by broadleaf stonecrop in bloom, Columbia Wilderness

Snow-flattened corn lilies, Bridge Creek Wilderness

Frost coats rabbitbrush on Brogan Hill, Malheur County

Lupine and paintbrush bloom below Mount Jefferson, Mount Jefferson Wilderness

Meadow of arnica wildflowers in full bloom, Steens Mountain, southeastern Oregon

"Sometimes you are walking: you begin / to know — even those things out of sight or hearing, / stones in the ground, flocks of birds / beyond the horizon. A little bit of snow forms in the sky: you feel it furring / out there, ready; then it comes down. / A quality of attention has been given to you: when you turn your head the whole world / leans forward. It waits there thirsting / after its names, and you speak it all out as it / comes to you; you go forward into forest leaves holding out your hands, trusting all encounters, telling every mile, 'Take me home.'"

— William Stafford, "For People with Problems About How to Believe"

Winter in Tims Creek Canyon, Camp Creek proposed wilderness

Penstemon grows from lava bed at McKenzie Pass, Three Sisters Wilderness

TREES

Oregon's diverse trees are best described as *elegant* and *stately*. In the mountains is the dense cover of evergreens, in the western valleys the symmetry of oaks, in the east the pungent aroma of juniper.

The maples that line many of our waterways not only help stabilize the soil, they also add beauty in the fall when they take on radiant hues of yellow, red and orange. Their leaves fall into the water and are carried downstream, creating streaks of color that rush past or get trapped in small whirlpools.

Evergreens are the giants of the northwest. Standing next to an old-growth fir in an ancient forest makes me think back on all the history that has taken place during its lifetime. Forest fires, storms and diseases have come and gone, yet it still stands. As I look around this living cathedral, I see death and rebirth: fallen trees whose rotting trunks and branches give life to young seedlings. I see a yew tree, which produces taxol, a cancer-fighting substance.

As I stand on the thick green carpet of moss that covers the forest floor, I look up to a canopy of intertwined branches. I am at peace here in this enchanted world, wondering how many more secrets man can unlock from these mystic, living giants.

Left: Dying noble fir tree, Mount Hood Wilderness
Above: Incense cedar trees, Umpqua National Forest, border of Rogue-Umpqua Divide Wilderness

95

"I rock high in the oak — secure, big branches —
at home while darkness comes. It gets lonely up here
as lights needle forth below, through airy space.
. . . noises drift up, and a faint
smooth gush of air through leaves, cool evening
moving out over the earth. Our town leans farther
away, and I ride through the arch toward midnight,
holding on, listening, hearing deep roots grow. . . .

Bullrun Rock viewed from Table Rock, Monument Rock Wilderness

. . . There are rooms in a life, apart from others, rich
with whatever happens, a glimpse of moon, a breeze.
You who come years from now to this brief spell
of nothing that was mine: the open, slow passing
of time was a gift going by. I have put my hand out
on the mane of the wind, like this, to give it to you."
— William Stafford, "Little Rooms"

Old-growth Douglas firs, Drift Creek Wilderness
Overleaf: Mountain hemlock beside rock slide, Mount Hood Wilderness

"It came when autumn came, the right day, / so clear and gold it shook us like a storm: / what the world promised had come, and we were / afraid. . . . / We didn't need any stars, only trees / with tops that leaned. . . . / We knew no harm would come, stopped by miles / and luck, with serene hills to stand / right where they did the most good. Hills are like that sometimes, near, to help. / No need, except for time, only a little space / to turn and move, as if calmly, on, steady, past leaves, past hills and roads, where we were going — away, and the end of the world."

— William Stafford, "Our Time"

John Day River flows beneath First Peak, Aldrich Mountains, Grant County

Fog drifts through forest of oak and ponderosa pine, Columbia River Gorge National Scenic Area, Wasco County

Snow-covered conifers, Middle Santiam Wilderness, Willamette National Forest

Ponderosa pines frame Palisade Rocks formation, Gearhart Mountain Wilderness

"
   . . . and oak with its fingers out in vain
   to hold nothing, then sigh. All that
   frozen country went under, winter
   only a sound, the pond a kettledrum.
   Children, events can find any face,
   and many as leaves are, a little weight
   at last will make them fall. . . . "
— William Stafford, "To the Children at the Family Album"

Aspen leaves on early snow, Mountain Lakes Wilderness

Early morning light on Douglas fir and cedar forest, Rogue River National Forest

"What's on the wall will influence your life,
they say; but erasing the wall will remind
everyone what was there. So a city
is troubled for years, and one of the ways
to live is to learn how to look away.
. . . But the trees not carved and walls undefaced
mean 'Not even Kilroy was here,'
and millions of us haven't killed anyone,
or a bear, or even an hour. We haven't
presumed. And — who knows? — maybe we're saved."
— William Stafford, "Graffiti"

Western spring beauty wildflowers and rotting logs, North Fork Umatilla Wilderness

Frost on ponderosa pine bark, Mill Creek Wilderness

"When we first moved here, pulled / the trees in around us, curled
our backs to the wind, no one / had ever hit the moon — no one.
Now our trees are safer than the stars, / and only other people's neglect
is our precious and abiding shell, / pierced by meteors, radar, and the
telephone. . . .
This message we / smuggle out in / its plain cover, to be opened
quietly: Friends / everywhere — / we are alive! Those moon rockets
have missed millions of secret / places! Best wishes. / Burn this."
— William Stafford, "An Oregon Message"

Hillside of larch in autumn, North Fork John Day Wilderness

Aftermath of a forest fire, Wallowa-Whitman National Forest
Overleaf: Aspen in Fish Creek Canyon, Steens Mountain

Technical Information

The images within this book were made with a Linhof Technika 4x5 field view camera, using lenses of 75mm, 90mm, 135mm, 150mm, 270mm, 360mm and 500mm focal lengths. An 81B filter was used in cloudy and shaded conditions to correct for the imbalance related to the blue dyes in the film. A polarizing filter was used at times to cut down on glare and at times to eliminate it completely.

Exposures were calculated with a Gossen Luna-Pro at metering values of 15 and 7.5 degrees. The length of the exposures ranged from 1/250 of a second to about three minutes. Apertures varied from f/5.6 to f/64. Ektachrome 64 and 100 Plus Readyload transparency films were used. The transparencies were separated by the printer on state-of-the-art laser-scanning equipment. Color reproduction was achieved with the goal of duplicating the image on film and accurately capturing the moment as it existed in time.

Acknowledgements

For their assistance and encouragement, I am very grateful to my son, Steve; my mother, Mary Terrill; my brother, Gervis Terrill; Dennis Johns; Larry Geddis; Yogi Rathod; Scott Kreuter; Brian Berger; Greg Krolicki; Larry Tuttle; Laura Sammarco; Jack Turner and all the others who have supported me throughout my career. I want to give special thanks to Laurie Hicks, for her patience and understanding.

Thanks also to the Oregon regional office of The Wilderness Society, the Portland Audubon Society, the Nature Conservancy of Oregon, my friends at Tryon Creek Photo Club, the Photographic Image Gallery, and Hans Matschukat and Jeff Gregor and their associates at PhotoCraft for developing my original transparencies with such great care. — S.T.

Snow on Yeon Mountain, Columbia River Gorge National Scenic Area, Mount Hood National Forest